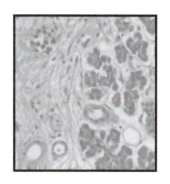

Diabetes

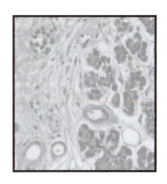

Diabetes

Margaret O. Hyde & Elizabeth H. Forsyth, M.D.

Franklin Watts
A Division of Scholastic Inc.
New York • Toronto • London • Auckland • Sydney
Mexico City • New Delhi • Hong Kong
Danbury, Connecticut

Cover design by Robert O'Brien
Interior design by Kathleen Hamilton

Photographs © 2003: AP/Wide World Photos: 66 (Stephan Boitano), 22 (J. Pat Carter), 32 (Paul Sakuma), 69; Corbis Images: cover, chapter openerss (Lester V. Bergman), 53 (Ed Bock), 58 (Andrew Brookes), 9 (Lou Chardonnay); Custom Medical Stock Photo/Reidlinger: 35; Harvard School of Public Health/Dr. Walter C. Willett: 46, 49; Hulton|Archive/Getty Images: 17; Joslin Diabetes Center, Boston MA: 71; Peter Arnold Inc./SIU: 34, 39; Photo Researchers, NY: 8 bottom (John Bavosi/SPL), 56 (David Gifford/SPL), 8 top right (Matthew Klein), 8 top left (Maximilian Stock LTD/SPL); PhotoEdit/Michael Newman: 23, 43.

Library of Congress Cataloging-in-Publication Data

Hyde, Margaret O. (Margaret Oldroyd)
    Diabetes / Margaret O. Hyde and Elizabeth Forsyth.
            p. cm.
    Summary: Discusses the causes of diabetes, who is likely to have this condition, how to prevent diabetic problems, and the search for a cure.
    Includes bibliographical references and index.
    ISBN 0-531-12209-3 (lib. bdg)   0-531-16607-4 (pbk.)
    1. Diabetes—Juvenile literature. [1. Diabetes. 2. Diseases.]
    I. Forsyth, Elizabeth Held.
    II. Title.

RC660.5 .H93 2003
616.4'62—dc21

                                        2002038033

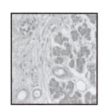 # Contents

CHAPTER ONE

What Is Diabetes?

When fourteen-year-old Shari found out she had diabetes, she decided to tell her friends. Most of them had heard of the disease, but they had some mistaken ideas about it. They said things like, "She got it from eating too much candy," and "I know someone who had it and he had to get *insulin* shots every day." They also said, "Shari's fun days are over," and "There goes her soccer playing." While most of these ideas are false, it *is* true that some people with diabetes need insulin shots—and it can be unpleasant.

Shari had been feeling very tired in the past few weeks, but she thought it was because she had been busy training for the swim meet, playing soccer, and staying up late doing homework. She was always very thirsty, and she seemed to be drinking constantly and using the bathroom a lot. She also noticed that she had lost weight, although she wasn't on a diet. Then one day, she woke up feeling awful and thought she might have the flu. She was weak and shaky, and she felt nauseated. Shari was so sick that her mother took her to the emergency room, where the doctor did a blood test. The test showed that she had too much sugar in her blood, an indication that she had diabetes.

Diabetes Is a Disease

At first, Shari found it hard to believe the doctor. She had heard of diabetes but knew little about it. She had some idea that it was connected with sugar because her grandmother called diabetes the "sugar disease." When her grandmother learned that

Shari had diabetes, she said, "I told her she would get 'sugar disease' if she didn't stop eating so much candy." But the disease is much more complicated than that. Having a high level of sugar in your blood is the result of having diabetes, not the cause of it. You should not feel guilty about having diabetes. It is not your fault.

If you have diabetes, your body does not properly use the

energy from the food you eat. Hamburgers, apples, potato chips, chocolate, and other foods are broken down inside your body into other forms, mostly into a kind of sugar known as *glucose* that the body uses for energy. Glucose needs insulin, a *hormone* that is released by the *pancreas*, an organ behind your stomach, in order to enter the cells. You might have plenty of glucose in your bloodstream, but without insulin, glucose

Hamburgers, chocolate, and other foods provide the fuel that our body needs for energy.

cannot get into your brain cells and other body cells for use as energy. Much as your automobile cannot move the gasoline in its tank to the engine if the key is not turned in the ignition, the body cannot use its food without insulin to let it in the cells.

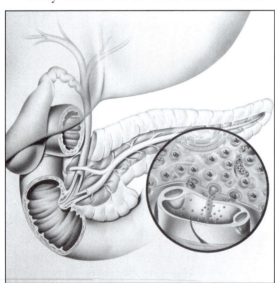

People with diabetes do not produce enough insulin inside their bodies. In some cases, no insulin is produced at all, or the insulin that is produced does not work properly. As a result, glucose builds up in the blood

This illustration shows the pancreas, with a close-up view of insulin production.

and overflows through the kidneys into the urine. When sugar enters the urine, water must go out with it. People with diabetes whose glucose is not under control are usually thirsty. They drink a lot of water to make up for the water that is lost in the urine.

There are three main kinds of diabetes. In type 1 diabetes, which is most common in young people, the body fails to produce enough insulin. In type 2, insulin is produced, but the body's cells cannot use it. The insulin cannot work to unlock cells for food to be used as energy. Type 2

Fluctuations in blood sugar may cause excessive thirst.

used to be called adult-onset diabetes, but so many children have it now that it is called type 2 or non-insulin-dependent diabetes. Type 3 diabetes is a kind of diabetes that can happen in pregnancy. Between two and five percent of all pregnant women in the United States develop it, and it usually goes away after the baby is born. The other kinds of diabetes are diseases that last a lifetime.

When people learn they have diabetes, many react with denial and anger. Some think it means they are going to die, but most people soon realize that although diabetes is a serious disease, it can be controlled. Shari's doctor told her about people who became famous in spite of having diabetes. There are famous ballplayers, tennis stars, TV stars, musicians, politicians, artists, and many others who achieved success in spite of diabetes. It has even been suggested that some of these people became great because the difficulties associated with diabetes forced them to persevere and be stronger than they would have been otherwise. The doctor told Shari that diabetes was nothing to be ashamed of. When Shari found out more about the disease, she was determined that she could be one of the millions of people with diabetes who have a good future.

Type 1 Diabetes

Shari was diagnosed with type 1 diabetes, a disease that used to be called juvenile diabetes or juvenile-onset diabetes because it usually starts early in life. People who have diabetes type 1 produce little or none of the insulin they need to convert food into energy. They lose weight because their bodies cannot use food properly.

Back in 1970, most doctors and researchers believed that type 1 diabetes developed suddenly. But during the next decade, they learned this was not true. A number of studies showed that the disease began as a slow process and probably involved *genes* and possibly a virus. Several genetic defects may be triggered into action by a viral infection.

When a virus or other foreign organism invades the body, the *immune system* goes into action to kill the virus. Type 1 diabetes is known as an *autoimmune disease*. An autoimmune disease is produced when the immune system turns against part of the body. It attacks the insulin-producing cells (called *islet cells*) of the body's own pancreas. This process begins long before there are symptoms of the disease. It may even begin soon after birth. For a time, the cells that have not yet been destroyed can still secrete insulin, but when too many insulin-producing cells have been destroyed, severe symptoms of diabetes appear suddenly.

Michael and Matthew are fifteen-year-old identical twins. Michael has diabetes type 1, but tests show that Matthew doesn't have any signs of getting the disease, even though he has inherited identical genes. Both brothers have genes that make them more prone to diabetes, but apparently Matthew has not been exposed to a virus or another environmental factor that acts with his genes to bring on diabetes type 1. In the general population, if one twin develops diabetes type 1, there is a 30 percent chance that the other one will also develop it.[1]

The symptoms of type 1 diabetes are:

- High levels of thirst
- Frequent urination
- Constant hunger
- Weight loss without dieting
- Blurry eyesight
- Extreme fatigue
- Nausea and vomiting
- Fruity odor of the breath

These symptoms usually develop rather suddenly, and they are severe. If not diagnosed and treated with insulin, the disease can worsen rapidly, and the person may go into a life-threatening coma. The first two symptoms are most common and are sometimes not recognized as a warning sign of type 1 diabetes.

Type 2 Diabetes

Jacob was sixteen years old when he found out that he had type 2 diabetes. Although Jacob didn't feel lucky after learning this, his doctor insisted that he was lucky to find out about his disease before it had time to do any damage. Like many other people with type 2 diabetes, Jacob didn't feel sick, but he got tired easily and seemed to be thirsty all the time. A blood test showed that the amount of sugar in his blood was too high. Jacob was overweight, and his father had type 2 diabetes; this helped the doctor to determine that Jacob also had the disease. At one time this kind of diabetes was uncommon in children, but the number of children who are found to have type 2 has tripled in the past five years. As more children become overweight, type 2 diabetes is becoming more common in young people.

When type 2 is diagnosed, the person's pancreas is usually producing enough insulin, but the body can't use the insulin properly. This is called insulin resistance. After a number of years, insulin production decreases, and the result is the same as in type 1 diabetes.

The symptoms of type 2 diabetes develop gradually. They are not as sudden or severe as in type 1. Symptoms may include:

- Tiredness
- Unusual thirst
- Frequent urination
- Blurred vision
- Weight loss
- Frequent infections
- Slow healing of sores

People with type 2 diabetes may be unaware they have it because their symptoms are mild. They may have it for years before it gets worse. Some people don't have any symptoms at all.

Jacob's body was not using insulin properly. The doctor said he would have to check his blood glucose regularly. He also needed to change his diet, lose weight, and exercise more, because eating a healthful diet and losing weight would make his body cells more sensitive to insulin. Jacob used to spend several hours every day watching television and snacking on chips, but now he plays basketball, and he has discovered that he likes it. He is getting used to eating fresh fruit and carrot sticks instead of chips as a snack. When he went for his checkup, the doctor was pleased to find that Jacob had lost weight and that his blood sugar was in the normal range.

Many people feel frightened, discouraged, and angry when they find out they have a disease that sometimes needs to be controlled by daily injections of insulin. It can be intimidating to learn that you are now suddenly responsible for keeping the disease under control for the rest of your life. In addition, you'll have to exercise, keep to a healthful diet, and not skip meals—no binging on ice cream or eating a whole box of cookies. Faithfully keeping to a routine like this is a challenge for people of any age, but most young people learn to deal with it amazingly well.

An Epidemic

Diabetes is becoming so common that it is considered a public health threat of epidemic proportions. In the United States, an estimated one in every 400 to 500 children and adolescents has type 1 diabetes. An estimated sixteen million people have type 2 diabetes; about one-third of these don't know they have it.[2] Another sixteen million people have "pre-diabetes," meaning the amount of sugar in their blood is gradually rising.[3] These people can greatly lower their risk of getting diabetes by walking thirty minutes a day and losing weight.

Everywhere in the world there are people with diabetes. More than 151 million adults now live with diabetes. That number is set to double in the next 25 years, according to Sir George Alberti, president of the International Diabetes Foundation.[4] Most people do not realize how serious diabetes is and how difficult it is to manage the disease.

CHAPTER TWO

The Discovery of Insulin

Bruce had a large dog named Bear who had grown rather fat. Bear seemed thirsty all the time and, because he drank so much water, it was not surprising that he had to go out about once every hour. It soon became clear to Bruce that something was wrong.

The veterinarian who examined Bear discovered that he had diabetes. He stayed at the animal hospital for a few days until the glucose level in his blood was normal. At home, Bear was put on a special diet, and his urine had to be checked every day. In the morning, Bruce followed Bear outside with a paper cup fastened to a stick to catch some of his urine. Using a test kit he bought from the vet, Bruce checked the dog's sugar levels. If the reading for sugar was too high, he injected insulin into Bear's muscles. This kept the dog alive for another two years.

Dogs played a major part in the discovery of insulin. For thousands of years, people who suffered from diabetes died early. In most cases, they lived only about a year or two after the symptoms were noticed. Diabetes was known as a disease about three thousand years ago. It was recognized by ancient Egyptians, Chinese, Hindus, and Greeks. The Greek physician Aretaeus, who lived in the second century A.D., gave diabetes its name, for the Greek word that means "pass through," or "siphon."[1] He observed that his patients who had diabetes seemed to "melt down" into urine. They became painfully thin. Although he did not know why at the time, it was because they lacked insulin in their blood that was needed for glucose to get into their cells.

In the eighteenth century, the word *mellitus*, meaning "honey," was added to the word diabetes to describe a sugary taste in the urine that is caused by the disease. The correct name for diabetes is diabetes mellitus. As long ago as 1500 B.C., the disease was recognized by pouring a patient's urine on the ground near an anthill. If the ants were attracted to the urine, the doctor knew it contained sugar and the patient had diabetes.[2] In the Middle Ages, medical experts called "piss prophets" used their senses of taste and smell to identify sugar in a patient's urine.

Late in the nineteenth century, two German scientists named Oskar Minkowsky and Joseph von Mehring studied the way fat was used in the body. They removed the pancreas from a dog who lived in the laboratory so it could be used to learn more about their experiments. The pancreas is a large gland behind the stomach that plays a part in digestion. Without its pancreas, the dog urinated again and again. The scientists tested the dog's urine for sugar and found that the dog had developed diabetes. From this, they realized there was a connection between diabetes and the pancreas, but no one could find what the connection was. They suspected that certain cells in the pancreas produced a substance that prevented diabetes. But how could it be isolated in a form that could be used to control the disease?

Doctors could not help the many patients who lost weight and died within a year or two after their diagnosis. They tried removing blood from their patients by bleeding them, and some gave their patients opium, a drug that relieved pain but was addictive. They told their patients to exercise and put them on various diets, including one that nearly starved them to death. Some of these diets helped slightly, but none controlled the disease. It took thirty years before someone was able to isolate the substance that was produced in the pancreas in a form that could be used to treat diabetes.

An Important Discovery

In the summer of 1921, two doctors, Frederick Banting and Charles Best, began their search for something that could control diabetes. They worked long hours without pay in a small room on the second floor of an old medical building in Toronto, Canada. They worked with dogs, searching for a substance that would control diabetes in the dogs so they could find something that would do the same in humans. By August, the researchers had isolated a substance from the pancreas that lowered abnormally high blood sugar in the dogs. A Canadian biochemist named James Bertram Collip helped to purify Banting and Best's extract, which later was called insulin.

In January 1922, the doctors were ready to try it on a human for the first time. Leonard Thompson was a fourteen-year-old boy who was dying of diabetes.[3] He was very, very thin, weighing just 75 pounds. He was the first to receive the extract, but he did not improve as much as was hoped. Twelve days later, after the extract was purified and made more active, the experiment was repeated. Soon Leonard began to gain weight, and with regular injections of insulin, he lived for thirteen more years before he died of pneumonia. Other trials followed with excellent results.

When Elizabeth Hughes developed diabetes in 1918, her doctor put her on a diet of 834 calories a day. She hated the diet and all who insisted on it, and she lost weight. Four years after her diagnosis, when Dr. Banting agreed to see her, she weighed just 45 pounds and could barely walk. Dr. Banting started her on insulin shots and increased her daily calorie intake. Soon she gained weight and appeared healthy. Those around her called this a "miraculous" transformation. Without the insulin, she would have died as a young girl. With it, she lived a happy and productive life.[4] She had about 43,000 insulin injections before she died suddenly of a heart attack at age sixty.

Charles Best and Frederick Banting pose outside Toronto University with one of the first diabetic dogs to receive insulin.

On May 3, 1922, John J. R. MacLeod, who supervised and helped to plan Dr. Banting's experiments, announced the discovery of insulin. MacLeod and Banting were awarded the Nobel Prize in 1923. Banting felt that Best, who had worked with him, should have been awarded the prize rather than MacLeod. Banting shared his prize money with Best, and MacLeod shared his money with Collip, who had purified the insulin.

The discovery of insulin has been called the beginning of modern medicine. Doctors could not cure the disease, but they could now treat people who would almost certainly have died from diabetes. Before 1956, there were no pills that helped people with type 2 diabetes to control the level of the glucose in their blood. Today there are a variety of medications.

CHAPTER THREE

Who Gets Diabetes?

Terry is a fourteen-year-old Pima Indian who lives in the Gila River Indian Community, south of Phoenix, Arizona. Terry is overweight and at risk for diabetes type 2. He belongs to a group of Indians who have the highest rate of type 2 diabetes in the world.[1]

The ancestors of the Pima Indians were among the first to set foot in the Americas about thirty thousand years ago. The Pima Indians have lived in the Sonoran Desert in southern Arizona for at least two thousand years. In the past, they grew wheat and Pima corn (corn that is lower in sugar than sweet corn), as well as many other foods that were good for their health. But when white people moved west, they diverted the Indians' water supply, and the Indians lost much of their food supply. The government gave them surplus food, such as lard, white flour, and other low-fiber, high-fat foods, and they grew fatter and exercised less. Today they eat much the same food as other Americans, many of whom are also fat and don't get enough exercise.

Researchers at the National Institutes of Health are studying diabetes among the Pima Indians and have been doing so for thirty years. They have a record of Terry's grandmother's and his grandfather's diabetes, and they know that four of his ten aunts and uncles also have diabetes type 2. Terry and his sisters are chubby, like many other children in his tribe. He is being encouraged to exercise and eat fruits and vegetables so that he will lose weight and be less at risk for diabetes.

Harold Osife, a Pima Indian, uses the exercise machine at the wellness center on the Gila River Indian Reservation. Osife was diagnosed with diabetes ten years ago.

Type 2 diabetes, once known as an "adults only" disease, has been growing much more common in children of American Indians, African Americans, Asians, and Latinos.[2] Some American Indian groups have extremely high rates of type 2 diabetes, but the rate varies with different tribes. It is not uncommon to find Pima Indian children as young as eight with diabetes type 2.

Latinos have a rate of diabetes that is two times higher than non-Latino whites. For every six white Americans who have diabetes, ten African Americans have the disease.[3] There has also been a dramatic rise in diabetes among Asians and Pacific Islanders who immigrate to America. Although these people are generally not as obese as Americans, they appear to have genes that make it especially likely for them to get the disease. When they come to America, they eat more fast food and junk food and exercise less than they did in their native lands. The chance that Asian Americans will develop diabetes and the number who have developed it is twice what it is for white Americans.

The Dangers of Obesity

Not all overweight people are diabetic. However, being fat increases the risk for diabetes because excess fat makes the body less able to respond to insulin. Losing weight by dieting and exercising gets rid of some body fat and increases the amount of muscle. This helps the body use insulin better.

Today, the rate of diabetes type 2 is much higher among all young people than in the past. More of them are fat today, partly because children watch more television and tend to get less exercise than their parents did when they were young. Children today also eat more fatty foods with fewer fruits and vegetables. This combination results in more fat children and more type 2 diabetes.

How can you tell if you are obese or just fat? An obese person is 30 percent or more over his or her ideal body weight. Obesity can be measured in a number of different ways, but calculating body mass index (BMI) is a common one. BMI is based

Many young Americans have unhealthy eating habits and inactive lifestyles, often leading to obesity.

on a formula that is a ratio between weight and height. Your school nurse or doctor can help you figure out what your body mass index is. Charts for young people are different from the charts for adults.

The rise in the number of overweight children has been called an epidemic by some health experts. Eric's mother received a letter from his school saying that he was at risk for diabetes because he was overweight. However, his mother did not see him as a fat child, and she did not think the school should be concerned about his weight. She would not have complained if she had been notified about a problem with his sight or his hearing, conditions in which anyone could recognize health risks. But schools say that controlling a child's weight is an important part of healthy living. Eric's mother took him to the doctor, who agreed that Eric needed to lose weight to prevent the risk of diabetes. In recent years, many schools have become involved with weight issues as a part of health education.

Ten percent of Americans under the age of seventeen are so fat that they can be called obese.[4] Some parents think their fat children will slim down when they are older, but most fat children become fat adults, and they are at high risk of developing diabetes. The prevalence of childhood obesity has doubled in the past thirty years and shows no signs of stopping.[5] Many preschool children who are fat already show the first signs of type 2 diabetes.

According to the Centers for Disease Control, rates of obesity surged 60 percent in the past decade, and one in five Americans is 30 percent above his or her ideal weight.[6] This epidemic of obesity is a great concern for those who are watching the nation's health. In the United States, Europe, and other places where most people have enough food to eat, the rich tend to be thinner than the poor. Many poor people eat too much food that is too high in fat and calories, such as chips, French fries, and cheeseburgers, while the rich eat more fruit and vegetables and exercise more. Obesity is becoming a problem in all parts of the world.

Many fat people are actually malnourished. In India, for example, in a survey of 83,000 women, 33 percent were malnourished. Of these, 12 percent were overweight or obese.[7] Filling up on starches such as rice, pasta, and bread can make a person fat without providing the vitamins, minerals, and other nutrients that the body needs.

Family Ties

Weight is not the only factor that determines diabetes. Scientists are not certain exactly how inheritance is involved, but they know that diabetes runs in families. In some cases of type 1 diabetes, there is a family member who has it, but type 2 is much more likely to run in families. If a person with type 2 diabetes has an identical twin, there is about an 80 percent chance that the twin will develop diabetes type 2. Even having a grandmother with diabetes may mean that you are at risk.

If young people know they have genes that may make them susceptible to diabetes, they should be sure to get enough exercise and be careful about what they eat. Studies show that exercise and diet play an important part in avoiding diabetes.

CHAPTER FOUR

Dealing with the Diagnosis

Sixteen-year-old Tyler couldn't believe what the doctor told him. He was shocked and scared to hear that he had this awful disease called diabetes that would never be cured. He would have to spend the rest of his life testing his blood and shooting himself with insulin. How was he going to continue playing soccer? How would his friends react? He thought that his life was ruined and he might as well be dead.

Tyler felt depressed and angry. He didn't want to learn about keeping track of his blood sugar or injecting insulin; he didn't feel like discussing a healthy diet with the nutritionist. He didn't want to think about anything. Instead, he wanted to pretend that he didn't have diabetes. But he soon realized that he had to deal with it, and he decided that the disease was not going to rule his life.

At first, Tyler didn't think about what his parents were feeling. They suddenly became overprotective, watching for low-blood-sugar reactions and fussing about eating his snacks on time. They worried that he might have an insulin reaction at school and that no one would recognize it. It seemed as though his mother and father were always nagging him about something. Tyler was annoyed until his parents explained that they, too, felt upset and worried when they learned about his diabetes. They kept reminding him to test his blood sugar and eat properly because they wanted to be sure that his disease was under control.

Tyler's parents were very understanding when he became frustrated and angry about his illness. But no one in the family thought of Tyler as sick or an invalid. He still had to do his share of the household chores, and he didn't get extra privileges. His parents treated him the same as his brother and sister.

Tyler was lucky. Sometimes parents of a young person with diabetes are so worried that they communicate their own fearfulness and pessimistic attitude to the diabetic, who then begins to think of him- or herself as sick and helpless. They often give him or her so much extra attention that everyone else in the family feels resentful.

Eddie was one of these teens. One day he came home while his brother Vinnie was watching television. Eddie switched the channel without asking, and Vinnie got very angry. He said he wished that Eddie would hurry up and die, because everyone did whatever Eddie wanted ever since he got sick.[1]

Staying in Control

Suzanne is a teenager who shared her story on an Internet site for young people with diabetes.[2] When Suzanne first found out about her diabetes, she kept her blood sugar under control, ate a healthful diet, and stayed away from junk food. Eventually, however, she became discouraged and lost her motivation. She began to cheat, thinking that just one candy bar wouldn't hurt. Soon she started snacking secretly more and more often. She also lied about her high glucose readings, making up normal readings to record in her daily log.

Suzanne felt guilty about cheating, so she avoided people. She lost interest in sports and other things that she had always enjoyed, and she no longer wanted to read anything about diabetes. When her parents and her doctor discovered what she had been doing, they forced her to listen to their lectures about the serious consequences of high blood sugar. Although she didn't like what they told her, Suzanne says it made her determined to get back her "control, motivation, strength, and power."

Suzanne's story is not unusual. Dealing with diabetes every day is not easy, and most people with this disease have cheated on occasion. They may write false numbers in their logbooks or exchange healthy lunch foods from home for cookies or candy at school. They might even change an insulin dose without telling anyone. Changing the amount of insulin or ignoring the need for glucose control can have serious or even fatal consequences.

Jed was responsible for testing his own blood sugar and giving himself insulin shots, but sometimes he couldn't resist the temptation to eat doughnuts or cake with his classmates. He then had to make up lower glucose readings to write in his log. Jed thought he had to lie because his parents always got angry with him if his glucose wasn't in perfect control all the time. Jed's parents expected too much from him, and he felt like a failure. But perfect control is not possible all the time. Even when the person sticks to his or her diet and does all the right things, stress and hormonal changes in teenagers can cause glucose readings to go out of control.

Sometimes, sixteen-year-old Rafael secretly gave himself extra insulin when he wanted to eat a large snack that wasn't in his diet plan. He didn't realize he could go into a coma or die from insulin shock. His blood-glucose levels were high because he was eating too much. When his parents found out about it, they made an agreement with him. Rafael would keep a record of all the food that he ate and of his insulin shots, and his parents would check the results of his blood tests. If he managed to reduce his blood-sugar readings and keep them down for two weeks, he would receive a bonus in addition to his regular weekly allowance. Rafael liked this idea because he was saving his money for a new guitar. Thinking about the reward made it easier for him to resist eating extra snacks.

Living with diabetes is difficult for people of all ages. But parents, brothers and sisters, doctors specializing in treating diabetes, nurses, dietitians, and counselors can make it easier to deal with this disease.

CHAPTER FIVE

Managing Diabetes

When the doctor explained to eight-year-old Adair that he had a disease called diabetes, Adair thought it sounded like "DIE-a-bee-tees," and so he believed that he was going to die.[1] That would have been true when his great-grandfather was a boy, but now the situation is very different. You can lead a long and active life even if you have diabetes. The goal of managing diabetes is to keep your blood sugar as close to normal as possible, because blood sugar that is too high or too low can lead to serious problems or even life-threatening conditions that need emergency treatment. Eating good foods, exercising, staying at a healthy weight, and taking your medicine help to keep glucose levels in a normal range.

> **If you have diabetes you need to remember four important things every day:**
> 1. Take your diabetes medicine.
> 2. Test your blood sugar.
> 3. Eat foods that are good for you.
> 4. Exercise.

Type 1 Diabetes

If you have type 1 diabetes, your pancreas does not make insulin, and you need to take insulin shots. When Carlos was diagnosed with type 1 diabetes, he was upset to hear that he needed injections every day. He knew that his grandmother takes pills for her diabetes, so why couldn't he take an insulin pill?

The doctor explained that his grandmother has type 2 diabetes and that her pancreas was still making some insulin; her pills are different and do not contain insulin. If Carlos swallowed insulin, his body would break it down and digest it before it got into his blood. The other problem is that the insulin molecule is too big to pass through the lining of the intestine. But researchers are making progress in getting around these obstacles.

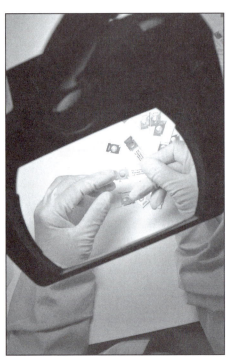

An engineer inspects insulin capsules to be used in an inhaler for diabetes patients.

Scientists have been testing insulin pills with a special coating that protects the insulin against stomach acid. Other researchers have been testing insulin with special molecules attached to it that help the insulin pass through the lining of the intestines into the bloodstream.[2] If this method is perfected, it could mean that someday Carlos and the other million or so people who have type 1 diabetes may be able to take insulin in pill form.

Or perhaps Carlos might get his insulin by breathing it, in much the same way that asthma medication is inhaled. Researchers are working to perfect ways of delivering insulin through an inhaler. When the insulin is inhaled, it is absorbed through the lining of the lungs into the bloodstream. These methods have been tested in people with type 1 and type 2 diabetes, and the results have shown some promise for the future.[3]

An insulin-containing skin patch is another development in the works. It is worn like a bandage and the insulin is absorbed through the skin over a period of twelve hours. Scientists are now working on a patch that delivers insulin for twenty-four hours.

At present, people with diabetes still have to take their insulin by injection, but there have been many advances since the middle of the twentieth century. All the insulin used at that time came from the pancreases of pigs and cattle, and it was not always pure or reliable. In 1947, when Bruce Beale was a child with type 1 diabetes, England was still suffering from the effects of World War II. He was sent to a hospital where there were shortages of medical supplies and properly trained nurses. The sanitary conditions were poor; there were no toilets and only a bucket for washing. The legs of the beds were placed in metal saucers full of disinfectant to keep fleas and lice from climbing into the beds. The needles that were used to inject insulin were huge and had to be cut down to size. Children sharpened their needles by rubbing them on a special stone, but the injections were still painful.[4] In 1950, people with diabetes could test their urine for glucose, but would have to wait until 1972 to test their blood glucose at home with a device called a glucometer.

Now, most of the insulin used is human insulin, not made from human pancreases but manufactured by a process called *genetic engineering*. The human insulin gene is inserted into harmless bacteria, and the gene then directs the bacteria to manufacture human insulin.

There are several different kinds of insulin, and they each work at different speeds. Some are very fast-acting and start working within a few minutes, and their effects last for a few hours. Long-acting insulin works around the clock with just one shot. Many people need to take two different types of insulin for good blood glucose control. They may take long-acting insulin in addition to a shorter-acting type before a meal. Most people with diabetes need at least two insulin shots per day for good control. Some people need three or four shots. It is very important for people who need insulin to take it every day and not skip any shots.

Not everyone responds in exactly the same way to insulin, so the doctor explained that Carlos would have to learn how the insulin works in his body. He would have to learn to time his shots to exercise times and mealtimes. How quickly or slowly insulin works depends on the kind and amount of exercise being done. Exercise helps insulin work better to lower your blood sugar. People with diabetes need to make sure that their blood sugar levels do not drop too low during strenuous exercise.

Its speed of action also depends on what part of the body is injected. The diabetes educator showed Carlos and his mother how and where to inject the insulin. Good places for injecting insulin are around the stomach, the outside part of the upper arms, and the outside part of the thigh. Insulin is absorbed at different rates in different parts of the body. Injections in the stomach work the fastest, and injections in the thigh work the slowest.

Carlos wondered whether he could learn to stick himself, but after some practice sticking needles into an orange, he gave himself a shot. He would no longer have to depend on someone else to give him injections. The shots are not painful because the needles are very thin and short and don't go far under the skin.

There are several devices that make it easier to inject insulin. For example, you can use an injector that automatically shoots a needle into your skin. Another device, the jet injector, shoots insulin so rapidly that no needle is even needed; the insulin stream goes right through your skin. Many people prefer using an insulin pen. It is like an ink pen with a needle instead of a tip and an insulin cartridge instead of an ink cartridge. The pen is convenient because you don't have to fill a syringe, and you don't have to carry a bottle of insulin when you are away from home.

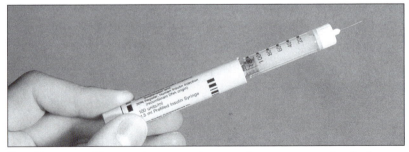

Insulin pens offer a safe, convenient, and accurate method of insulin delivery.

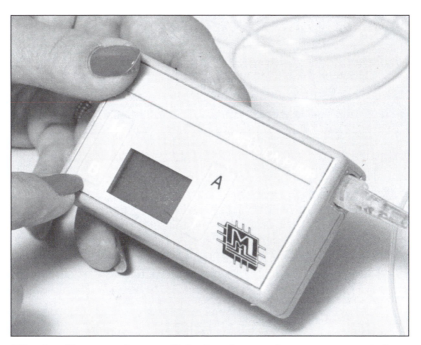

The insulin pump is a small device that can be worn or carried. It continuously delivers small amounts of insulin.

A different way of taking insulin is the insulin pump. This is a small, computerized device about the size of a cell phone that delivers a continuous flow of insulin. It is programmed to deliver a basal rate, the amount of insulin needed when one is not eating. The person using it can send extra boosts of insulin before meals or whenever more insulin is needed. A predetermined amount of insulin is given for the food that is eaten. The insulin flows from the pump through a plastic tube that is connected to a needle inserted under the skin with the end of the plastic tube taped in place. The pump runs on batteries, and it can be worn clipped to a belt or in a pocket. A pump is not for everyone, however. It is expensive and it takes a lot of practice to get used to it. Also, it is not foolproof, and you still need to test your blood sugar. But a pump can give you better control of your blood sugar, and it allows you to get insulin by pushing a button instead of filling a syringe and injecting yourself.

Type 2 Diabetes

Type 2 is the kind of diabetes that more often affects people over the age of forty and is most common in adults over 55, but young people can get it, too. This form of diabetes usually begins with insulin resistance, a condition in which fat, muscle, and liver cells do not use insulin properly. At first, the pancreas keeps up with the added demand by producing more insulin, but as time goes on, it loses the ability to secrete enough insulin, so blood sugar levels start to rise. Being overweight and inactive increase the chances of developing type 2 diabetes. About 80 percent of people with type 2 diabetes are overweight. In addition, they often have elevated blood pressure and high cholesterol.

Some people who have type 2 diabetes need medicine in order to lower their blood sugar, even if they eat the right foods, watch their weight, and exercise every day. After a few years, their bodies may not use insulin properly, and then they will have to take diabetes pills or insulin. If you have diabetes and get sick with the flu or some other infection, your blood sugar may be more difficult to control. If you take pills for diabetes, the pills may not control your blood sugar as well while you are sick, so you may need to take insulin injections temporarily in order to keep your glucose levels in a good range.

There are several kinds of medicines for people with type 2 diabetes. Each kind works in a different way to help lower blood sugar, including:

- Stimulating your pancreas to make more insulin
- Decreasing the amount of sugar that your liver makes
- Slowing the rate at which your body absorbs starches (foods such as bread, cereal, pasta, and potatoes)
- Making your body's cells more sensitive to insulin

If you take pills to lower your blood sugar, you should know that pills are not a substitute for a good meal plan and exercise. You can't pig out on French fries and cheeseburgers and expect the medicine to do all the work. You should always take your pills exactly the way your doctor prescribes them; for example, some medicines need to be taken with meals. Don't skip doses. Also, some medicines have side effects. Sometimes side effects can be serious. Nick's medicine made him feel weak and dizzy, and he had trouble breathing, so the doctor changed his medications. Alicia was taking the same medicine, but she experienced only a mild stomach upset that went away after a few days. Weight gain, ankle swelling, liver disease, and low blood sugar are other side effects that may occur with some diabetes medicines.

Pre-Diabetes

Donna was overweight and didn't like sports or other physical activities. When she found out that her blood sugar was higher than normal, she became concerned, even though she was a healthy fifteen-year-old. She worried because she is a member of the Pima Indian tribe. She knew that half the adults in her tribe have diabetes, and that almost all of those with diabetes are overweight. Both of her parents and many of her other relatives had diabetes.

The doctor told her she might be able to lower her blood sugar by losing weight, eating healthful foods, and exercising regularly. She was very conscientious about following the meal plan that her doctor prescribed, and she tried to avoid eating foods with lots of fat and carbohydrates. She started taking long walks every day. As a result, she lost weight and her blood sugar went down to normal. Donna was considered pre-diabetic—a person likely to develop diabetes. There may be as many as 16 million people with pre-diabetes in the United States. It is estimated that most of these people will develop type 2 diabetes in the next decade.

If your blood glucose is higher than normal, but lower than the diabetes range (called pre-diabetes), your chances of getting type 2 diabetes increases. You are also more likely to get it if you are overweight and have one or more specific risk factors (see sidebar on page 38). In addition, you are at increased risk of developing heart disease. In the past, many people have been told that they had "borderline diabetes," but the guidelines have changed. Doctors now know that people with higher blood sugar levels are no longer considered normal but are at risk.

Doctors use two tests to diagnose pre-diabetes. One test measures fasting glucose (the amount of blood sugar after the person has fasted for 8 to 12 hours). The other test is the oral glucose tolerance test or OGTT, in which the fasting blood sugar level is measured, and then measured again two hours after drinking a solution containing glucose. Normal fasting glucose is below 110. People with pre-diabetes have impaired fasting glucose—levels between 110 and 125. If blood glucose is between 140 and 199 two hours after drinking a glucose solution, the person has pre-diabetes. Normal blood glucose is less than 140 two hours after drinking. If fasting blood sugar is 126 or more, or the OGTT shows blood sugar levels of 200 or more, the person has diabetes.

The good news for people with pre-diabetes is that they can reduce their risk of developing type 2 diabetes by 58 percent if they lose even a modest amount of weight and get regular exercise. If you weigh 200 pounds, losing just 10 pounds can make a difference.

Your Risk for Type 2 Diabetes

- Having a parent, brother, or sister with type 2 diabetes
- Family background is African American, American Indian, Asian American, Pacific Islander, or Latino
- Having had diabetes during pregnancy
- Blood pressure of 140/90 or higher
- Cholesterol levels not normal, i.e. HDL ("good" cholesterol) is lower than 35 or triglycerides more than 250[5]

Testing Your Blood Sugar

It's a nuisance to keep sticking yourself with needles, but it's important to test your blood sugar regularly if you have diabetes. You must keep your glucose levels from getting too high or too low because both of these conditions can make you seriously ill.

People with diabetes need to test their blood at least twice a day, and sometimes as often as four to seven times a day. Carlos also had to go to the doctor every three months for a different kind of blood test called the hemoglobin A1c test. When glucose binds to the hemoglobin in red blood cells, glycohemoglobin is formed. By measuring for glycohemoglobin, the hemoglobin A1c test shows how much sugar is sticking to your red blood cells. Red blood cells have a life span of about three months. So the test shows what your average blood sugar was for the last three months and is an accurate indication of what your blood sugar is most of the time. Treatment is aimed at keeping your A1c below 7 percent. (For people who do not have diabetes, it is about 5 percent).

Researchers are trying to find new ways of testing blood glucose without needle sticks. In 2002, the Food and Drug Administration approved one such device for children and adolescents, after having approved it for adults in 2001. Called the

Testing Blood Glucose Levels

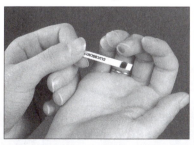

If you have diabetes, you will probably need to buy a test kit that will measure the level of glucose in your blood. The kit uses a drop of blood on a small strip that is placed in a meter to measure the level of glucose. In some kits, the drop of blood is obtained by sticking your finger with a spring-operated lancet that comes with the kit. There are new types of kits that use a very small amount of blood that can be obtained from your arm. These are helpful for people who must use them often.

GlucoWatch, it is worn like a watch, and it measures glucose painlessly through the skin six times an hour. The device sounds an alarm if glucose reaches dangerous levels. However, it is not a perfect solution, because it must be used along with occasional finger-stick tests for exact measurements of glucose levels.[6]

What if you could measure your blood sugar by shining a light in your eyes? It might be possible. Scientists at CIBA Vision, a contact lens manufacturer, have been testing a special contact lens that measures the glucose in tears. Molecules in the lens attach to the glucose. Shining a light into the eyes produces a glow in the lens, and a device measures the amount; the more glucose that is present, the more fluorescence there is.[7] The problem of measuring blood glucose accurately without drawing blood presents many difficulties, but researchers have been testing a number of different methods. The ideal device would monitor blood sugar accurately and continuously and would have an alarm to warn of low glucose.

High Blood Sugar

High blood sugar can cause long-term problems. If you have had diabetes for a number of years, you are at risk for diseases of the eyes, kidneys, blood vessels, nerves, teeth, and gums. But if you keep your blood sugar under control you may be able to prevent these problems. Researchers at the National Institute of Diabetes and Digestive and Kidney Diseases (NIDDK) studied more than 1,400 people with type 1 diabetes over a period of ten years. One group was given intensive therapy to keep their blood sugar as close to normal as possible. The researchers found that this group had a much lower chance of getting eye, kidney, and nerve disease.[8] The aim was to try for pre-meal levels of 70-120, and less than 180 after eating. See Chapter 7 for more about problems that can result from diabetes.

High blood sugar (*hyperglycemia*) usually develops slowly, when you do not have enough insulin in your body. If you eat too much, if you don't take your medicine, or if you don't get enough exercise or are stressed, your blood sugar can go up. Illness such

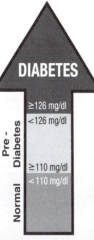

What Is a Good Blood Sugar Level?

Everyone has some sugar (glucose) in his or her blood. The normal amount of sugar is between 70 and 110 milligrams per deciliter (mg/dl) in people who do not have diabetes. Your blood sugar goes up after you eat, but goes down in a couple of hours if you do not have diabetes. This is not the case in people with diabetes; their blood sugar stays high even if they haven't eaten for hours. The aim of taking pills or insulin is to keep blood sugar levels as close to normal as possible. If you have diabetes, a good range is between 80 and 110 mg/dl before you eat. Two hours after a meal, your sugar should be less than 150. Seventy is too low and more than 180 is too high. (A word of caution—everyone is different, so 80 may be too low for some people.)

as the flu, an infected finger, surgery, or stress can all cause high blood sugar. Sometimes, even if you have done everything right, your blood sugar can get too low or too high.

The doctor said it was important for Carlos to test his blood regularly. If he was sick with the flu or had vomiting or diarrhea, he would have to test more often. If his blood sugar remained over 240 for more than a day, he should call the doctor right away.

In addition to testing his blood, he would also have to do a urine test if he was sick or if his blood sugar was more than 240. Carlos would need to test his urine for *ketones*. Your body makes

Symptoms of High Blood Sugar

These are the warning signs of high blood sugar:

- Tiredness
- Thirst
- Blurry vision
- Faintness, nausea, or vomiting
- Frequent urination
- Abdominal or stomach pain

this chemical when you don't have enough insulin, and it spills out in your urine. This condition, known as *diabetic ketoacidosis*, can make you very sick and can even cause death if it is not treated. If your urine test shows ketones, it is important to call your doctor immediately. Symptoms of ketoacidosis are vomiting, weakness, fast breathing, abdominal pain, and a sweet smell on the breath.

Low Blood Sugar

Your blood sugar can drop too low if you take too much insulin, miss a meal, exercise too much, or drink too much alcohol. Low blood sugar (*hypoglycemia*) can happen suddenly, and it needs to be treated quickly.

Carlos took his insulin one morning and then skipped breakfast because he was late for school. He knew that this was not a good idea, because insulin lowers the blood sugar whether or not you eat. He started to feel shaky and light-headed in class about an hour later, and he realized that he was probably having a low blood sugar reaction. So he quickly ate a few pieces of hard candy that he always carried with him.

At the first sign of low blood sugar, Carlos immediately ate something with sugar in it. Hard candy, orange juice, regular soda sweetened with sugar (not diet soda), a tablespoon of sugar

---

Symptoms of Low Blood Sugar

Low blood sugar is a medical emergency that can be life-threatening if not treated quickly. These are the symptoms of low blood sugar:

- Shakiness
- Tiredness, sleepiness, or hunger
- Headache or sweating
- Anxiety, irritability, or anger
- Acting withdrawn
- Confusion, fainting, or seizures if blood sugar drops very low

---

or honey, and special glucose tablets are some fast-acting foods that combat low blood sugar. If you have diabetes, you should always be prepared for a low-blood-sugar reaction by keeping some sugary food handy wherever you go. You should tell your family, friends, and teachers how to recognize the signs of low blood sugar and how to treat it. If your sugar gets very low and you become confused, you might not be able to help yourself. Wearing a medical identification tag that says you have diabetes and lists your medicines can be a lifesaver. The tag can be worn as a necklace or bracelet.

Emergency medical professionals are trained to look for medic alert tags such as these.

A policeman saw sixteen-year-old Joshua stagger down the street and then fall down. He had passed out and couldn't answer any questions, and at first the officer thought he was drunk. But when he noticed Joshua's identification bracelet and read the information on it, he realized that Joshua was having a very dangerous low-blood-sugar reaction. He called 911, and when the ambulance arrived, the emergency medical technician gave Joshua a shot of *glucagon*. Glucagon is a chemical that raises blood sugar quickly. It is not needed often, but it is very useful in an emergency, when blood sugar is very low and the person is unconscious or cannot take anything by mouth.

Recognizing low blood sugar is sometimes difficult. Young children who act cranky and tired may be experiencing a low. Sometimes, when lows occur at night they cause bad dreams and stomachaches, or headaches in the morning. When this happens, the doctor may change the dose or timing of the insulin shots and may suggest increasing the amount of food in the regular nighttime snack.

Hypoglycemia unawareness is a condition that may happen after people have many lows over a period of time; after a while, the warning signs start to disappear. The more lows there are, the less the warning, and the greater the risk.[9]

CHAPTER SIX

Healthy Eating and Exercise

If you had lived two hundred years ago and had diabetes, you might have been on a diet of rancid milk, pork, animal fat, and bread. Some doctors prescribed medication that caused vomiting and diarrhea. Other treatments of long ago included fasting every other day.[1] Fortunately, things are very different now. We know that the foods that are good for people with diabetes are good for everyone. Diabetics don't need special foods, but they do need a special meal plan.

The Food Pyramid

When fifteen-year-old Kim got diabetes, the doctor introduced her to a dietitian who helped her and her mother plan meals that everyone in the family would enjoy. The dietitian told her about an eating guide called the food pyramid, which was devised by the United States Department of Agriculture and recommended for everyone by the Department of Health and Human Services in 1992. The pyramid is divided into six groups and it helps you to choose a variety of healthy foods.

According to this pyramid, the foods at the bottom should make up the major part of your diet, while the foods at the top should be eaten sparingly. Together, all these foods provide the three main nutrients that the body needs: protein, fat, and carbohydrates. The guidelines for people with diabetes are essentially the same, except that in the diabetic diet plan, beans are included with starches at the bottom instead of with protein foods.

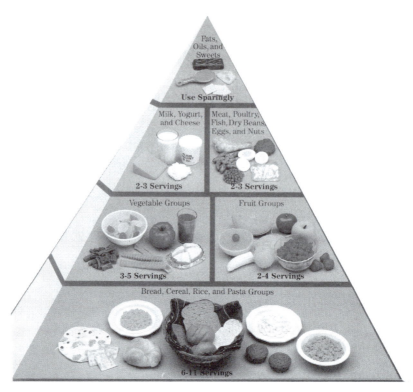

The USDA food pyramid is used as a general guide for a diet low in fat and high in nutrients.

Starches make up the largest part of the pyramid at the bottom. They include bread, cereal, pasta, beans, rice, and starchy vegetables. The dietitian told Kim to eat two servings of starch at every meal. Starches such as brown rice and beans are better choices than pasta or white bread.

Fruits and vegetables are just above starches on the pyramid; they have lots of vitamins and minerals and not many calories. Above the fruits and vegetables are dairy foods and protein foods such as meat, chicken, fish, eggs, and tofu. Kim learned that she had to cut back on these foods. She also learned that fish and chicken breast are better choices than red meat. Most people in the United States eat much more protein than they need. The dietitian said that the largest part of her diet should consist of the two bottom layers of the pyramid—starches, fruits, and vegetables.

46

At the very top of the pyramid are fats and sweets; you should eat only small amounts of these foods even if you don't have diabetes. Not all fats are the same. Animal fat and fat from dairy products (saturated fats) raise your *cholesterol* and should be eaten in limited amounts. Trans fatty acids—another kind of fat that is found in many margarines and baked goods—are also bad for you because they raise cholesterol. Unsaturated fats, which are present in fish and plant oils such as olive, corn, and canola, are much better choices because they reduce the level of cholesterol in your blood and lessen the chances of heart disease when they are substituted for saturated fats.

Carbohydrates include starches and different kinds of sugars. Starches are large, complicated structures made up of glucose molecules. Some foods, such as fruits, vegetables, and milk, contain various kinds of natural sugars. Most of these starches and sugars are broken down into glucose in the body. Most of the glucose in your blood comes from the carbohydrates that you eat. Kim was surprised to find out that foods like potatoes and pasta—starches—are broken down in the body and end up as glucose.

It is true that the level of sugar in your blood rises when carbohydrates are broken down into glucose, but not all foods have the same effect on your blood sugar. The way your blood sugar responds depends on a number of things, such as how the food was prepared and what other foods you eat with it. Some foods

---

Is Sugar Bad?

Everyone had told Kim that she would have to give up foods like ice cream and cake forever, but sugar is not as bad as people used to think. Kim was happy to learn that she could include some sugar in her meal plan so she could have an occasional treat. She learned why she couldn't eat all the cake and cookies she wanted, because all the starches and sugars are turned into glucose in her body. The dietitian explained that sugar has calories, but it doesn't have much nutritional value. Candy is another example of a food with empty calories. Eating too many sugary foods would require having to cut down on more nutritious carbohydrates such as cereal and grains.

contain more carbohydrates than others do. Some are broken down into glucose faster than others are. For example, cooked food is digested faster than raw food. Glucose is released into the blood more slowly from carbohydrates that take a long time to break down. Food made up of whole grains, brown rice, and beans break down more slowly than foods made with refined starches such as white rice and white flour. For this reason, the dietitian suggested that it would be better for Kim if she ate less pasta and potatoes and more whole grains. Kim experimented with unfamiliar foods and discovered that she liked brown rice—a healthier choice—better than white rice. There is no single diabetic diet that fits everyone's needs. Each person with diabetes needs a personalized plan, because everyone is different.

Sweeteners

Sugar is not always labeled as sugar, so you need to read the nutrition facts on food labels. Sucrose is regular table sugar. Molasses, beet sugar, cane sugar, brown sugar, confectioner's sugar, powdered sugar, and maple syrup are basically sucrose. Other kinds of sugars are fructose, lactose, maltose, and sugar alcohols, which are sorbitol, mannitol, and xylitol. Some artificial sweeteners that have been approved by the Food and Drug Administration are saccharin (Sweet and Low), aspartame (Nutrasweet and Equal), sucralose (Splenda), and acesulfame potassium (Sweet One). Artificial sweeteners do not raise your blood glucose level, but they should still be used in moderation.

Some New Ideas

Dr. Walter Willett of Harvard University and other researchers have criticized the government recommendations for healthy eating. They say that the USDA food pyramid does not make enough of a distinction among the different kinds of carbohydrates, such as between refined starches and whole grain foods. For example, a serving of white bread is not equal to a serving of oatmeal. He and some other researchers theorize that a diet high in refined starches may make people more prone to

Healthy Eating Pyramid

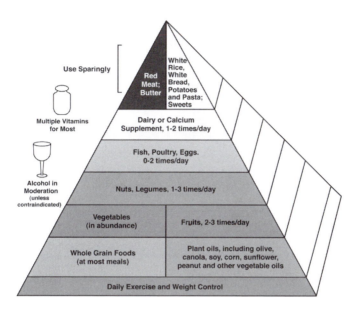

Use Sparingly

Multiple Vitamins for Most

Alcohol in Moderation (unless contraindicated)

Red Meat; Butter

White Rice, White Bread, Potatoes and Pasta; Sweets

Dairy or Calcium Supplement, 1-2 times/day

Fish, Poultry, Eggs. 0-2 times/day

Nuts, Legumes, 1-3 times/day

Vegetables (in abundance)

Fruits, 2-3 times/day

Whole Grain Foods (at most meals)

Plant oils, including olive, canola, soy, corn, sunflower, peanut and other vegetable oils

Daily Exercise and Weight Control

Dr. Walter Willett of Harvard University has created a new food pyramid, which reflects the most recent advances in nutrition and health research.

diabetes and heart disease because they cause a rapid rise in blood glucose. These are known as foods with a high glycemic index. Researchers emphasize the point that whole grain foods release carbohydrates more slowly than refined grains and that this prevents blood glucose from spiking.

Dr. Willett also thinks that the USDA food pyramid does not place enough emphasis on the differences between animal fats and plant oils. Saturated fat, which comes from meat and dairy products such as whole milk and butter, should be limited. You should also avoid trans fatty acids, which are found in some vegetable shortenings and some baked products. But unsaturated fats found in vegetable oils, nuts, and fish do not raise cholesterol and are much better for you. Dr. Willett's own food pyramid recommends more plant oils, placing them at the bottom of his pyramid. He agrees that red meat and butter are to be eaten very sparingly and keeps them at the top of his pyramid, along with refined starches such as white bread, potatoes, and pasta.[2] The Department of Agriculture is studying these recommendations in preparation for replacing the old USDA pyramid with a new one that will reflect the latest scientific research.

Balanced Meals

Kim was confused and discouraged at first because she thought she would never learn how to balance her meals and snacks with her insulin shots. She didn't know how to keep track of how many calories she was eating. She didn't even know what a serving of food was supposed to mean or whether she could substitute one food for another. The dietitian explained that she could exchange one food for another in the same food group. She also had to learn more about the size of portions.

It was easy to follow these guidelines at home, but what if Kim was eating at a restaurant? She also had to learn how to choose healthful foods when she was away from home. The dietitian gave her some helpful tips. For example, a serving of

---

Fast Food Choices

Kim and her friends like to go to fast-food restaurants sometimes. Below are two typical fast-food meals. Which one should Kim order?

Meal #1 — a cheeseburger with French fries, cola, and ice cream

Meal #2 — grilled chicken on a whole-wheat bun, salad with low-fat dressing, fruit juice or low-fat milkshake, and low-fat frozen yogurt

Answer:
Meal # 1 is tempting, and it has nutritious foods — meat, cheese, and dairy — but it is loaded with saturated fat, sugar, and calories.

Meal #2 is a far better choice for everyone because it has much less fat and it includes vegetables and fruit.

---

steak (4 ounces uncooked) is about the size of a deck of cards. A small apple is one serving of fruit, and one banana is equivalent to two servings.

Kim realized that she didn't have to feel weird or different just because she has diabetes. She *does* have to be more careful than most people about what and how much food she eats. She also has to remember not to miss meals or snacks, no matter what she is doing or where she is. Kim's mother had always served her family healthful foods, so Kim had an easier time adjusting. Instead of junk food, she was already accustomed to having a piece of fruit, peanut butter and crackers, or some left-over beans as an after-school snack. Kim doesn't drink soda very often; she usually drinks fruit juice or low-fat milk. If she wants, she can drink diet soda, which contains sugar substitute and no sugar. She can even treat herself to an occasional ice cream or other sweet dessert.

Diabetes can be more difficult for very young children, especially at school or on special occasions such as Halloween and birthday parties. Lots of parents prepare for times like this by substituting other special treats for candy or cake. School can present problems for the child if the teacher doesn't know much about diabetes.

Fortunately, most teachers understand that children with diabetes are like everyone else, except that they need to be careful about eating at the proper times, taking their insulin, and watching for low and high blood sugar. They try not to single out the child with diabetes, but find ways to make them feel part of the larger group. For example, some teachers who have diabetic students set aside a snack period for all the students to accommodate the one child who needs it.

There are many books and Web sites where you can get helpful tips about how young people have managed their diabetes. On some Web sites, you can find a pen pal and read accounts written by children and teens with diabetes, telling about the challenges they have faced and inviting others to share stories. These sources are listed at the end of this book.

Exercise and Other Physical Activity

Millie has diabetes. She is an overweight couch potato. She doesn't exercise except for walking her dog around the block twice a day. Although she doesn't have any other health problems, Millie behaves as if she were an invalid. She thinks she should not exert herself because she has diabetes, but she is wrong. Exercise is good for everyone.

Spike and Bo Loy are brothers who were diagnosed with type 1 diabetes when they were very young. They didn't allow their disease to stop them from doing anything. They both excelled in school and at sports and have trekked in Africa, backpacked around the world, and enjoy surfing and snowboarding. They also wrote a book called *Getting a Grip on Diabetes* (see page 92) that might inspire Millie to get off her couch.

Exercise is especially good for people with diabetes because it helps keep weight down and helps insulin work better to lower blood sugar. You might even be able to use less insulin or eat more when you work out. It gives you more energy, and it is good for your heart and lungs. You should exercise regularly several times a week—walking, swimming, riding a bicycle, hiking, participating in sports, or working out in a gym are all good activities that help burn calories and get rid of fat. If you have diabetes, you should talk with your doctor to make sure that you have no problems that might prevent you from doing certain kinds of exercise.

Matt was diagnosed with type 1 diabetes; he was on the track team and wondered if his disease would prevent him from running. The doctor told him he could continue everything he had been doing before he got diabetes, but he had to follow a few important rules. He had to eat before he exercised, and check his blood sugar before and after running. The doctor said that exercise would lower his blood-sugar levels, but if he exercised for a long time, his blood sugar might drop too low. He would have to plan on eating a snack during exercise to prevent hypoglycemia.

Moderate, daily exercise can help maintain control of diabetes.

Exercising at night is not a good idea if you have diabetes, because it could cause low blood sugar during the night. Your blood-sugar levels can drop as long as twenty-four hours after you exercise. If your blood sugar is high—more than 240—you should not exercise. Matt always wore an identification bracelet saying he had diabetes, and he always carried hard candies and a snack in case of low blood sugar.

People with type 2 diabetes can benefit from exercise because it makes their bodies more sensitive to insulin and because it helps them lose weight. If you have type 2 and don't take pills or insulin, your blood sugar will not get too low when you exercise. If you do take pills or insulin for type 2, dangerously low blood sugar is not likely, but you should watch for it.

Diabetes should not prevent anyone from exercising. Will Cross, a 35-year-old with type 1 diabetes, completed a 730-mile (1,175-km) walk to the South Pole on January 17, 2003.[2] He pulled a sled loaded with food and gear, demonstrating that diabetes does not prevent such efforts. The walk also helped to raise funds for diabetes research. Will is living proof that people with diabetes can excel in all kinds of challenging activities, including mountain climbing, skiing, and skydiving.

CHAPTER SEVEN

Preventing Problems

Too much sugar in your blood for a long time causes problems in many parts of your body. High blood sugar can damage the heart, blood vessels, kidneys, nervous system, skin, and eyes. If you have diabetes, you may develop problems in any of these areas or perhaps none at all. Some people with diabetes mistakenly believe that no matter what they do, they will develop complications. So why bother with the nuisance of checking blood sugar several times a day and watching everything you eat? The truth is that the risk of developing a complication is largely decreased with the proper control.

As noted in Chapter 5, researchers found that when people with diabetes kept their blood sugar as close to normal as possible, complications were slowed or prevented. The people in these studies had to test their blood and inject insulin more often, and they had to make more adjustments to match their insulin dosage to their eating and exercise. After ten years, the researchers found that the group of people who kept this very strict control of blood sugar reduced their risk of diabetic eye problems by 76 percent compared to the group who did not use such tight control. Kidney disease was reduced by 39 to 54 percent, and nerve disease was reduced by 60 percent.[1]

Heart and Blood Vessels

Your heart is a big muscle that pumps blood throughout your body through large blood vessels called *arteries* and smaller vessels called *capillaries*. Blood carries oxygen to every part of your body. Other blood vessels called *veins* return blood to the heart. Sometimes blood vessels become narrowed or clogged up, making it harder for the blood to get to the cells in your body. Tissues that are deprived of oxygen and nutrients may become damaged or die. This can happen in your heart, brain, and other places in your body.

Having diabetes changes the chemistry of some substances in the blood. It can cause an increase in your blood cholesterol. Your body makes cholesterol, and it is also found in some animal foods that we eat. When cholesterol is too high, it causes the insides of large arteries to become narrowed or clogged. This condition is called *atherosclerosis*.

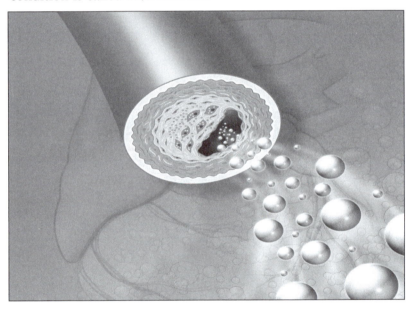

This drawing shows a coronary artery that has been partially blocked by atherosclerosis, which can cause chest pain or a heart attack.

Chest Pain

George Miller has had diabetes for many years, but he wasn't always careful about keeping his blood sugar in control. The meal he most liked was a big steak and fried potatoes, and his favorite snacks were pizza and ice cream. These foods contain lots of saturated fat and cholesterol. After a test showed that the cholesterol in his blood was high, his doctor said he could lower it if he cut down on fatty foods—the ones at the top of the pyramid.

One day as he was rushing to catch a bus, he felt a pain in his chest. It went away when he sat down, but it came back again two days later when he was mowing his lawn. The arteries to George's heart were narrowed, and his heart wasn't getting enough blood whenever it had to work harder, such as when he ran for the bus. The chest pain it caused is called *angina*. Angina is a warning that the vessel may become completely clogged.

If a blood vessel in or near the heart becomes completely blocked, the blood supply to that part of the heart is cut off and the muscle gets damaged, with the result that the heart becomes weaker. This is what happens when someone has a heart attack. Like angina, a heart attack causes chest pain, and the person may also feel sweaty, weak, and nauseated.

High Blood Pressure

Narrowed blood vessels can cause high blood pressure or hypertension. High blood pressure affects more than half the people who have type 2 diabetes. High blood pressure makes your heart work harder. If someone has heart, eye, or kidney problems from diabetes, hypertension can make them worse. If you have

More than 50 million American adults have high blood pressure. It can affect your brain, eyes, arteries, kidneys, and heart.

hypertension, there are medicines you can take to lower your blood pressure. Losing weight, eating more fruits and vegetables, and avoiding salty foods also help to lower blood pressure.

Stroke

You may know an older person who has had a stroke and was left with weakness on one side of his or her body. A stroke happens when part of your brain doesn't get enough blood and stops working. The signs of a stroke vary, depending on what part of the brain has been damaged.

These are some warning signs of a stroke:

- Sudden weakness or numbness of an arm, leg, or the face on one side of the body
- Sudden trouble talking or understanding, or confusion
- Sudden dizziness, loss of balance, or trouble walking
- Sudden trouble seeing, or seeing double
- Sudden severe headache

Sometimes one of the warning signs happens and then it goes away. This called a *transient ischemic attack*, or TIA. Anyone who gets any of these warnings should be taken to the doctor or the emergency room immediately. Prompt treatment may prevent serious damage.

Legs and Feet

Maria's grandmother had diabetes, and she didn't know why she began feeling pain in her legs after she walked only one block to the supermarket. The doctor explained that the blood vessels in her legs had become narrowed, and not enough blood was getting to the muscles. Walking or doing exercise brings on this kind of pain, which is called *intermittent claudication.*

The Nervous System

Your nerves carry messages between your brain and the rest of your body. There are different kinds of nerves. For example, some nerves send messages to your heart, lungs, and intestines, telling your body what to do without your even being aware of what is happening. Other nerves send messages to your brain. If you are walking on the beach and stub your toe on a rock, the nerves in your foot send a pain message to your brain.

Having high blood sugar for a long time can damage your nerves so that they don't send signals or send them too slowly or at the wrong time. High blood sugar may damage the covering of the nerves, or it may interfere with the blood supply to the nerves. This kind of damage to the nervous system from diabetes is called *diabetic neuropathy*. However, nerve damage is not always due to diabetes; there are other conditions that may cause it.

The nerves that go to the arms, hands, legs, and feet are called *peripheral nerves*. Damage to these nerves can result in feelings of numbness, burning, tingling, "pins and needles" sensations, or pain.

Autonomic nerves go from your spinal cord to your stomach, intestines, lungs, heart, bladder, and sex organs. They regulate parts of your body that are not under your voluntary control. They regulate your heartbeat and blood pressure. Damage to these nerves can make your heart beat too fast or too slowly. Or you could get dizzy when you stand up, because the nerves can't keep your blood pressure steady. Some autonomic nerves go to the digestive system. If these are damaged, food might pass through your stomach and intestines too quickly or too slowly, causing nausea, constipation, or diarrhea. If nerves to the bladder are affected, it might be hard to tell if your bladder is full and you need to go to the bathroom. Damage to autonomic nerves can also cause problems with having sex.

If a person has had diabetes for a long time, it doesn't necessarily mean that he or she will have these complications. If some problems do happen, doctors have ways of making them better and preventing them from becoming worse.

Kidneys

Your kidneys are organs that filter waste from your blood. An artery brings blood into the kidney, where tiny filters called *glomeruli* clean the blood. The waste and extra fluid go out into the urine through a tube called the *ureter*. You have two kidneys; each kidney has a ureter, which carries the urine into the bladder. The cleaned blood goes out of the kidney and back into the bloodstream through a vein.

Many people with diabetes develop kidney problems after many years, but not everyone who has diabetes will get complications. The two most important ways to prevent problems are to keep blood sugar and blood pressure as close to normal as possible. The study mentioned earlier showed that people who kept their blood sugar under tight control reduced their chance of kidney disease by as much as 54 percent.

High blood pressure and high blood sugar damage the glomeruli, so that protein leaks out of the kidneys into the urine. The kidneys become less efficient at filtering out waste and extra fluid, so they build up in the blood instead of going out into the urine. Kidney failure from diabetes happens very slowly, so you might not feel sick for many years. There may be no signs until the kidneys have almost stopped working. Then you may feel very tired and weak all the time, you might feel sick to your stomach, and your face, hands, and feet may get puffy and swollen from a buildup of fluid in your body.

An early sign of kidney damage is finding small amounts of a protein called *albumin* in the urine. This is a silent sign that you cannot see or feel. If you have diabetes, your doctor will probably check your urine at least once a year to make sure your kidneys are working properly.

Eyes

Damage to several parts of the eye is a common complication for people who have had diabetes for a long time. The most common problem is damage to the *retina*. The retina is the lining at the back of your eye, which acts like film in a camera that records images coming into the eye. The tiny blood vessels in the retina are damaged by high blood sugar and high blood pressure. This condition is called *diabetic retinopathy*.

This condition causes the blood vessels to swell and weaken, and then become clogged. New blood vessels grow, but they are weak and break easily, allowing blood and fluid to escape into the eye. The blood interferes with vision, and you might see spots or everything may look dark. Later, scar tissue may form on the retina, and it may tear away from the back of the eye. When this happens, you might see spots or flashing lights. Other signs are blurred or double vision, or pain in your eyes. If the retina becomes detached you might lose your sight unless it is treated immediately.

Damage occurs slowly, so you might not notice any problems with vision at first. Beginning changes can be detected by an eye examination in which drops are used so that the retina can be seen clearly. It is important for people with diabetes to have regular eye exams, because the damage can be slowed or stopped if it is discovered in the early stages. Laser treatment is used to seal off leaking blood vessels in the retina and slow down the process. Keeping blood sugar normal is very important for preventing diabetic retinopathy. The study mentioned earlier found that the people who kept tight control of their blood sugar decreased eye damage by 76 percent.

People with diabetes are also more likely to get two other eye problems: cataracts and *glaucoma*. A cataract is a clouding of the lens of the eye, and it interferes with vision, making everything look fuzzy. The lens with the cataract can be removed by surgery and a new lens put in its place. Glaucoma is increased pressure in the eye, which can damage the optic nerve and cause blindness unless it is treated. Treatment consists of the use of special eye drops that lower the pressure.

Infections

When you have high blood sugar, you have a greater risk of getting an infection. The white blood cells of your immune system attack viruses, bacteria, and other organisms that cause infections, but too much sugar interferes with their activity. To make matters worse, the extra sugar feeds the germs. Although people with diabetes are more prone to infections anywhere in their bodies, certain areas such as the feet and mouth need special care.

Foot Problems

There are two problems that could develop in your feet. If you have diabetic neuropathy (damage to the nervous system), for example, you might not feel a blister on your foot and it might get worse because you don't know it is there. Or, if you have peripheral vascular damage (the narrowing of blood vessels in the arms and legs), the decreased blood going to your legs and feet makes it more difficult for sores or infections to heal.

Sometimes, even a small blister on your foot could turn into a bad sore that doesn't heal. Instead, it keeps getting deeper and may even reach down to the bone. The tissue gets infected and dies; it turns black and smells bad. This is called *gangrene*, and it is very serious. In order to stop it from spreading, the doctor may have to cut off a toe or foot or even amputate part of the leg. But there are many things people with diabetes can do in order to avoid this problem.

If you have diabetes, you need to wash and dry your feet every day. You also need to check for sores and blisters and make sure that your toenails are properly trimmed. It is important to wear shoes that don't rub or squeeze your feet.

Teeth and Gums

Lots of people have tooth and gum problems. If you don't brush and floss every day, a sticky film of germs called plaque builds up on your teeth. Your gums become red and bleed when you brush your teeth, and the gums may pull away from the teeth. Eventually, the bone becomes infected, and your teeth may become loose or sensitive. More people lose their teeth from gum disease than from cavities.

High blood sugar can make gum disease worse. People with diabetes need to control their blood sugar, take good care of their teeth, have regular dental checkups, and watch for signs of gum problems. If you have diabetes and take good care of yourself, you can avoid or slow down many of the problems that can happen later in life.

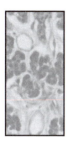

CHAPTER EIGHT

Searching for a Cure

Cory was two years old when he developed type 1 diabetes. Now that Cory is four, he is used to having his blood sugar checked every day. The insulin shots that keep him alive are part of his daily routine. When his parents prick his finger for a drop of blood to measure his blood sugar at night, he raises his arm without opening his eyes. Over a period of two years Cory has had more than four thousand finger pricks and almost three thousand insulin injections. He has to have six to ten insulin shots a day, depending on his activities. His parents watch every bit of food he eats, and they work opposite shifts so that one of them can always be with him. Cory's parents hope a cure will be found soon so that he does not need insulin shots every day for the rest of his life.

Stem Cell Research

Cory's mother joined a group of mothers who are trying to persuade Congress to allot more money for diabetes research. She wrote to her senator asking him to support research that uses stem cells to help find a cure for diabetes. Cory's parents and more than one million people in the United States who have type 1 diabetes—along with their families and friends—hope for a cure. Then there would be no more finger sticks, insulin shots, or insulin pumps.

Stem cell research is one of the most exciting possibilities for a cure for diabetes type 1. Embryonic stem cells are cells that form in a mother's body when an egg is fertilized. Normally, these cells multiply into a healthy baby. Many women who want babies but cannot have them turn to specialists who develop embryos in a laboratory. They use reproductive cells taken from a man and woman who hope to become parents. After these cells are combined in the laboratory, the doctors put a few of these embryos into the mother's body. Chances are good that one of the embryos will develop into a baby. Many embryos are left over in the lab from this procedure, and these are usually frozen in case the parents want to use them later. If they are not used by the parents, they may be given to scientists for medical research.

Because embryos can grow into babies when put in the mother's body, not everyone agrees that embryos should be used as a source of stem cells for medical research. Some people think that this use is destroying human life. Other people think that using them is preserving human life because the embryonic stem cells are used to learn how to prevent or cure diseases such as diabetes.

In August 2001, protesters against stem cell research demonstrated across from the White House. They wanted the president to ban embryonic stem cell research.

Embryonic stem cells can be made to turn into any kind of cell in the human body. Scientists have been able to turn these cells into islet-like cells that produce some insulin when they are placed in the bodies of mice.[1] Someday they may be able to use stem cells in people with diabetes to replace non-functioning insulin-producing cells of the pancreas. One of the problems is finding a way to make one body accept cells that are produced by another. Someday, adult stem cells taken from the diabetic person's own body may be able to supply the insulin a person needs, but the embryonic stem cells hold more promise.

New Genes

The search for a cure for diabetes goes on in many different ways. In one kind of experiment, scientists used genes, or strands of *DNA* that contain the molecules that carry genetic information. They were able to put *genes* in the intestines of mice where they made insulin. If this experiment is shown to work safely in a large number of mice, it may then be tried on human volunteers. If all goes well, about fifteen to twenty years after the discovery in the laboratory and after numerous experiments on animals and people, this kind of experiment may be approved for general use in people with diabetes type 1.

Recent research supported by the Diabetes Research Institute Foundation involves changing genes in muscle cells so they can produce a chemical, proinsulin, that is formed in the body before insulin is formed. Further research might find a way to get the body to produce insulin.

Pancreas Transplants

If a person has a pancreas that does not work, why not put a new one in his or her body? Surgeons first transplanted a working pancreas from someone who died into a person with diabetes in 1966. They have performed more than ten thousand pancreas transplants worldwide since then. More than one thousand pancreases are transplanted each year in the United States.[2]

Although this can be successful, there are problems. Pancreas transplants require major surgery, and not enough pancreases are available for everyone who needs one. Another problem is the potential rejection of the new organ by the immune system of the person who receives the pancreas. When the immune system recognizes the new pancreas as a foreign invader, it tries to destroy it. This is called rejection, and it happens to anything strange in the body, whether it is a virus that causes a cold or a new organ such as a pancreas. Drugs to prevent rejection are given to the patients who have transplants before and after the operation, and the patients may have to take these drugs for the rest of their lives.

Most people who opt for a pancreas operation also need a kidney transplant, and both transplants are done at the same time. Kidney failure is one of the most common complications of diabetes, as noted in Chapter 7.

An Artificial Pancreas

Scientists have been trying to produce an artificial pancreas for more than thirty years. They are trying to wrap *islet cells* in a membrane that would prevent the immune system from attacking them. It would release insulin the way a normal pancreas does naturally, in response to blood-glucose levels. This would work to keep the amount of glucose in the normal range. A device that will work like an artificial pancreas to signal when the body needs insulin and deliver it in precise doses is being developed by scientists at the Department of Energy's Lawrence Livermore National Laboratory in partnership with a company named MiniMed Inc. It offers diabetic patients new hope for a more normal lifestyle.[3]

Islet Transplants

Each pancreas contains several million islet cells. Why not just put them in the body of a person with type 1 diabetes where they can continue to make insulin? Islet cells are very delicate, so they can be easily damaged when they are taken from a donor's

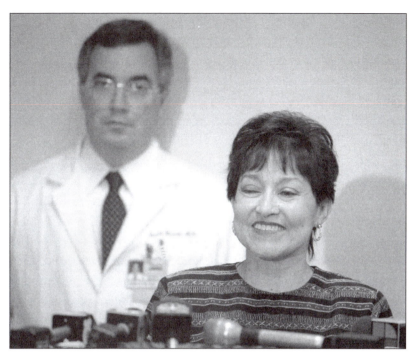

Islet cell transplant patient Marta Herrera spoke at a press conference in 1996. Hers was the country's first successful case of reversed type 1 diabetes using purified islet cells.

pancreas. However, researchers have found a chemical that helps them gently remove islets from a donor's pancreas. Islets form only about 2 percent of a pancreas. Until recently, it took as many as 5 or 6 pancreases for one person, but Dr. Camillo Ricordi, director of the Diabetes Research Institute, developed a new method that makes it possible to get enough islets for one operation from just one pancreas. In spite of this, there is still a shortage of islets for transplant.

The success rate of islet transplants was very low until recently. In the summer of 2000, Dr. James Shapiro and his team in Edmonton, Alberta, Canada, reported that they had found a way of performing transplants that involves fewer drugs to prevent rejection of the new islet cells. He also uses fresh rather than frozen islet cells. This "Edmonton Protocol" is a procedure that is now being explored in many trials around the world.

Consider a case that is typical of transplant patients. Ken suffered from diabetes type 1 for thirty of his forty years. Before he agreed to have islet cells from a healthy pancreas injected into his body, Ken's doctors warned him that he might still have to take insulin because not all operations are successful. Ken began taking medicine before the operation to prevent his own cells from attacking the new ones, as they would with any foreign cells.

Ken carried a pager so that he could be reached quickly when the cells became available for his operation. At the hospital, he was given medicine to help him relax. Then a doctor told him to hold his breath while he inserted a large needle into a place on Ken's back just below his ribs. The needle was inserted so that the new cells were injected into a vein that is connected with Ken's liver. On a screen that looks like a television, Ken watched the new cells dribbling into the vein. The injection took forty-five minutes. Later, the operation was repeated so more islet cells could be added. The new cells seemed to work almost immediately. Ken no longer needed insulin shots.

Ken said he felt fantastic soon after the operation. He did not mind taking vitamins, antibiotics, and pills to keep his body from rejecting the new cells. All of this seemed easy after the blood-sugar tests and insulin injections he previously had to take. He knew that there were risks of his body not being able to defend itself against infections or cancer, but he was willing to take those risks. No one knows how long the transplanted cells will continue to produce insulin.

Doctors are doing experiments similar to Ken's in about twenty medical centers in the United States. Others in Canada and Europe are also experimenting with islet cell transplants in efforts to help patients with type 1 diabetes. Scientists are experimenting with enclosing the islets in a capsule to protect them against rejection when they are inserted in the body of a patient. They are also testing different drugs to protect the transplanted cells against rejection. They hope to find a way to overcome this problem without the need for a person to take anti-rejection drugs over a lifetime. Dr. Gordon Weir and others at the Joslin

Dr. Gordon Weir is well known in the field of diabetes research. He specializes in islet cell transplantation.

Diabetic Center in Boston, Massachusetts, have demonstrated that encapsulated islet cells transplanted into mice can survive and function for more than a year.[4]

If scientists are successful in perfecting islet transplants, the number of patients who have islet transfusions will increase. But the number will be limited by the cost of the operation—about $100,000—and by the fact that islet cells are relatively scarce. Someday, scientists may be able to use islet cells made from stem cells. Then there would be enough for everyone.[5]

Although the islet transplants work soon after the operation, no one knows how long they will continue to do so. In some patients who had them for more than a year, the transplants have begun to fail. When this happens, the patient must return to insulin.

Drugs

Just about everyone with diabetes hopes that insulin pills will soon replace shots. When insulin is swallowed, it is broken down by stomach acids. Researchers from Purdue University are trying to develop a pill that changes size and shape depending on the amount of acid around it. The pill coils up in the stomach, where there is a lot of acid, and it releases insulin in the small intestine, where there is less acid and where it can be absorbed without being destroyed. Much remains to be done before such a pill will be ready for consumer use. Some researchers believe that insulin will never work in pill form because so many factors affect blood-glucose levels and because the correct amount of insulin varies with the food one eats.

In another approach, scientists connected with a company known as GMP Companies, Inc., in Fort Lauderdale, Florida, have been successful in treating diabetic animals. Using a drug called INGAP Peptide, they have stimulated the insulin-producing cells in newly formed islet cells in the animals' pancreases. Now they are trying this drug on people in special trials, but it may be many years before they know for sure if it is safe.[6]

One exciting new approach to preventing the destruction of the cells that produce insulin is the use of monoclonal antibodies in newly diagnosed patients. An antibody is a chemical produced in the body to fight foreign invaders such as viruses and bacteria. Monoclonal antibodies are those made in laboratories for special purposes. Dr. Jeffrey Bluestone at the University of California at San Francisco and researchers at some other laboratories are exploring the use of a monoclonal antibody known at OKT3. This drug has stopped or slowed down the progressive destruction of insulin-producing beta cells for more than a year. Some of the children in the drug trial retained high levels of insulin production for more than two years. The results of these tests appear promising, but many more people must be tested before the results are certain and the procedure reaches doctors' offices.

A Vaccine

The search for a vaccine to prevent type 1 diabetes is taking place in a number of laboratories. Researchers in the United States and Australia are working together to search for a vaccine for type 1 diabetes. Scientists in Israel have developed a vaccine that keeps the immune system from destroying the pancreatic cells that produce insulin. The drug, called DiaPep277, is being tried on people at various centers around the world. Three injections over a period of six months were successful in preventing the disease from getting worse in some newly diagnosed patients. But the drug needs to be tried in many more people to learn if it really works.

In another approach, scientists are working on producing a vaccine by injecting genetic material into potato plants. The vaccine has been shown to affect the newly formed islet cells in experimental mice. Potatoes are being grown that carry many kinds of vaccines for other diseases, so it does not seem strange that scientists would be experimenting with them in trying to find a vaccine to protect the insulin-producing cells of the pancreas.[7]

Although there is no vaccine or cure for diabetes today, researchers hope that they are on the verge of finding one. Everyone who knows something about diabetes hopes that this will happen soon.

People with diabetes sometimes become overwhelmed with the disease and its care. This condition is known as diabetes burnout. Dr. Lawrence Chan of Baylor College of Medicine in Houston, Texas, who does research on gene therapy and diabetes, tells patients not to lose hope. Better things are happening.

CHAPTER NINE

Myths About Diabetes: Sorting Fact From Fiction

On a separate piece of paper, mark the numbers of the following statements as true or false. The answers begin on page 77.

1. Sugar causes diabetes.

2. You can catch diabetes.

3. There is a herbal remedy for type 2 diabetes.

4. People with diabetes can't play sports or go to camp.

5. As long as you feel OK, your blood sugar doesn't matter.

6. A doctor takes care of your diabetes.

7. "Bad diabetes" is the kind where you take insulin.

8. Blood testing is only for people with bad diabetes.

9. All diabetes is inherited.

10. If you start taking pills or insulin, you can eat anything you want.

11. Pills for diabetes are oral insulin.

12. People with diabetes should avoid parties.

13. If you get diabetes as a child, you may outgrow it.

14. Insulin cures diabetes.

15. Most people know the difference between type 1 and type 2 diabetes.

16. People who have diabetes can eat as many "sugar-free" foods as they want.

17. People with diabetes will die young.

18. People with diabetes can never have children.

19. People with diabetes can't have their ears pierced.

20. Aloe juice is a substitute for insulin.

21. People diagnosed with diabetes can never eat sweets again.

22. A piece of fudge can kill a person with diabetes.

Answers:

1. False.

Sugar doesn't cause diabetes. But eating too much of any food, including sweets, can cause you to gain weight. A positive family history, obesity, and not being active can put you at increased risk for diabetes.

2. False.

You cannot catch diabetes.

3. False.

There are no herbal or natural remedies for diabetes. The best natural remedy is a healthy diet and exercise.

4. False.

There are special camps for people with diabetes and they are very successful. If you are looking for a camp, check the Web at www.childrenwithdiabetes.com/camps/index.htm. At this site, you can read about various camps across the country.

5. False.

When blood sugar is above normal, you don't know it without a blood test. As many as a third of people who are diabetic don't know they have the disease.

6. False.

A doctor can give you instructions about how to care for diabetes, but you are responsible for your own care.

7. False.

All kinds of diabetes are serious diseases.

8. False.

Everyone with diabetes should test blood sugar every day.

9. False.

Ten percent of children with type 1 diabetes have a family history of diabetes. Type 2 diabetes tends to be an inherited trait.

10. False.

Good control of blood sugar means following a healthy meal plan and exercising in addition to taking pills or insulin.

11. False.

Pills for diabetes are not oral insulin. Insulin taken as a pill would be destroyed by stomach acids. New research holds promise for a coated pill that may protect insulin so it can be taken orally.

12. False.

Parties are good for people with diabetes. They help to reduce stress. However, the meal plans must be carefully followed, even at parties. Adults with diabetes should ask their doctor if it is safe to have a drink that contains alcohol. Alcohol can cause a low-blood-sugar reaction.

13. False.

People do not outgrow diabetes.

14. False.

There is no cure for diabetes. Insulin helps the body to maintain the correct level of glucose in the blood.

15. False.

In countries throughout the world, even in developed nations where most people are well educated and medical care is good, many people do not understand that diabetes is a serious disease, and they do not know the difference between the two types of diabetes. For example, in Ireland, many people believe that diabetes is a disease of adults and that it is easily taken care of with pills. They don't realize that type 2 is a serious disease. Many Japanese people associate diabetes with laziness and overeating, so they tend to keep the disease a secret from everyone except family members. In the United States, attitudes are more open and people tend to talk more readily about an illness such as diabetes. This openness makes it easier for everyone to learn the facts about diabetes and to correct any misconceptions.

16. False.

Many "sugar-free" foods are high in calories. They may also contain compounds known as sugar alcohols, which can raise blood sugar. Starchy foods such as potatoes and bread are changed into sugar in the body and can raise blood sugar.

17. False.

If you take good care of yourself and keep your blood sugar under control, you can greatly reduce the risk of diabetes-related problems later in life.

18. False.

Women with diabetes can get pregnant and have healthy children.

19. False.

You can have your ears pierced. Ear piercing should always be done under sterile conditions, but people with diabetes need to be especially careful about avoiding infections.

20. False.

There is no substitute for insulin.

21. False.

Your diet can include occasional sweets, but they should be eaten in moderation, and not at every meal. All carbohydrates raise your blood sugar, but sweets such as candy are empty calories because they do not provide nutrients that are found in carbohydrate foods, such as bananas or beans.

22. False.

A single piece of fudge will not kill you, but it is hard to eat just one piece.

Notes

Chapter One

1. Holly Schachner, M.D., "Type 1 Diabetes: What Is It?" prodigy.healthology.com/focus_article.asp?f=diabetes&c -diabetes_type1.

2. American Diabetes Association, National Diabetes Fact Sheet, www.diabetes.org/main/info/facts/facts_natl.jsp

3. American Diabetes Association, Pre-Diabetes, www.diabetes.org/main/info/pre-diabetes.jsp.

4. "Diabetes Affects 1 in 20 World-wide," news.bbc.co.uk/1/hi/health/1005664.stm.

Chapter Two

1. American Diabetes Association, *Complete Guide to Diabetes* (New York: Bantam Books, 2000), 28.

2. Robert Dinsmoor, "The History of Diabetes," 216.167.3.245/kids/searchforacure/2000/05/history.html.

3. "Canadian Medicine: Doctors and Discoveries," www.mta.ca/faculty/arts/canadian_studies/english/ about/study_guide/doctors/insulin.html.

Chapter Three

1. Gretchen Becker, *Type 2 Diabetes* (New York: Marlowe and Company, 2000), 208.

2. Randi Hutter Epstein, "An Epidemic in the Making," *Yale Medicine* (autumn 2001), 32–36.

3. National Diabetes Information Clearinghouse, "Diabetes in African-Americans," www.niddk.nih.gov/health/diabetes/pubs/afam/afam.htm.

4. American Association for the Advancement of Science, "The Fat of the Lands," *The Economist* (February 23, 2002), 81.

5. Health World Online, "Prediabetes Prevalent Even in Preschoolers," www.healthy.net/asp/templates/news.asp?Id=4367.

6. Epstein, 32.

7. "The Fat of the Lands," 81.

Chapter Four

1. Pat Kelly, *Coping with Diabetes* (New York: The Rosen Publishing Group, Inc., 1998), 108.

2. Suzanne, "Diabetes 123 and Children With Diabetes," www.childrenwithdiabetes.com/kids/d_02_1e1.htm

Chapter Five

1. Carol Antoinette Peacock et al., *Sugar Was My Best Food* (Morton Grove, Ill.: Albert Whitman and Company, 1998), 9.

2. Terri Kordella, "The Future of Insulin," *Diabetes Forecast*, March 2003.
    www.diabetes.org/main/community/forecast/march2003/future.jsp.

3. Jennifer B. Marks, M.D. "Diabetes Management in the Future: A Whiff and a Long Shot?" *Clinical Diabetes* vol. 16, no. 3 (1998), 140.

4. Bruce Beale, The History of Diabetes,
    www-unix.oit.umass.edu/~abhu000/diabetes.beale.html.

5. "Am I At Risk for Type 2 Diabetes?" National Diabetes Information Clearinghouse.
    www.niddk.nih.gov/health/diabetes/pubs/risk/risk.htm#7.

6. "FDA Approves Glucowatch Device for Children With Diabetes," FDA News, August 27, 2002,
    www.fda.gov/bbs/topics/NEWS/2002/NEW00830.html.

7. "Pitt Researchers Develop Non-Invasive Glucose Sensor That Can Be Worn As a Contact Lens," UPMC News Bureau,
    www.upmc.edu/NewsBureau/medsurg3/glucose_sensor.htm.

8. National Institute of Diabetes and Digestive and Kidney Diseases, "Diabetes Overview,"
    www.niddk.nih.gov/health/diabetes/pubs/dmover/dmover.htm.

9. Francine Kaufman, M.D. "Preventing Hypoglycemia (Low Blood Glucose) in Children," *Diabetes Forecast* 52 no. 6, (1999): 77-79.

Chapter Six

1. Pat Kelly, *Coping With Diabetes* (New York: The Rosen Publishing Group, Inc., 1998), 49.

2. *Harvard Public Health Now,* August 24, 2001, "Nutrition Book Author Willett Rebuilds USDA Food Pyramid," www.hsph.harvard.edu/now/aug24.

3. Bob Karlovits, "Local Team Reaches South Pole," *Pittsburgh Tribune Review*, January 18, 2003.

Chapter Seven

1. *American Diabetes Association Complete Guide to Diabetes,* 2nd ed. (Port City Press, 1999), 295.

Chapter Eight

1. "Stem Cells: Scientific Progress and Future Research Directions," Department of Health and Human Services, June 2001, www.nih.gov/news/stemcell/scireport.htm.

2. Jason Socrates Bardi, "Weighing the Risks and Benefits of Xenotransplantation," www.scripps.edu/newsandviews/e_20020923/xeno.html.

3. Sue Gano, "Working Science: Artificial Pancreas," www.pnl.gov/energyscience/06-01/ws.htm.

4. Research Highlights, Annual Report 2001, Boston, MA: Joslin Diabetes Center, p. 4.

5. University of Maryland Medicine, "Islet Cell Transplantation May Soon Be An Alternative for Patients With Type 1 Diabetes," www.umm.edu/future/islet_cell.htm.

6. The Diabetes Institutes Foundation, "INGAP Research Reaches Human Trials," www.dif.org/news_articles/ingap1202.shtml.

7. "Potent Potato Diabetes Vaccine," www.newswise.com/articles/1998/9/potato.nbt.html.

 # Glossary

albumin—A protein. Finding more than a normal amount of albumin in the urine may be an early sign of kidney damage.

angina—Pain that is caused when the heart muscle is not getting enough blood due to the narrowing of one or more arteries that supply the heart muscle.

arteries—Large blood vessels that carry blood away from the heart to other parts of the body.

atherosclerosis—A condition in which there is a buildup of fat in large and medium-size arteries. This causes the arteries to become narrowed or clogged, and it can slow down or stop the blood flow.

autoimmune disease—Disorder of the immune system in which the immune system mistakenly attacks and destroys body tissue that it believes to be foreign.

autonomic nerves—Nerves that regulate body functions that are not under your voluntary control, for example breathing, blood pressure, and movement of food through the digestive tract. They go from the spinal cord to your stomach, intestines, lungs, heart, bladder, and sex organs.

calorie—A unit used to measure the energy that comes from food. Different foods have different amounts of calories. For example, vegetables have few calories, and fats have a lot. People with diabetes need to follow meal plans that tell them how many calories and what kinds of food to eat at each meal.

capillaries—The smallest of the body's blood vessels. Capillaries have very thin walls, so oxygen and glucose in the blood can pass through the walls into the cells, and waste products from the cells can pass back into the blood.

carbohydrate—One of the three main classes of foods and a source of energy. Carbohydrates are sugars and starches that the body breaks down into glucose, which is a simple sugar that the body needs to feed its cells. The body is not able to use carbohydrates for energy if it does not have enough insulin or if it cannot use the insulin it has. This is what happens in diabetes.

cataracts—Clouding of the lens of the eye that interferes with vision.

cholesterol—Fatty substance found in blood, muscle, liver, brain, and other tissues. The body needs some cholesterol and makes it. Too much cholesterol can cause fat to build up in the walls of arteries and slows or stops the flow of blood. Some foods, such as egg yolks and butter, contain a large amount of cholesterol.

DNA (deoxyribonucleic acid)—Chemical substance inside the nucleus of a cell that carries genetic information.

diabetic ketoacidosis (DKA)—Severe, out-of-control diabetes with very high blood sugar, resulting in a buildup of ketones in the body. Signs are nausea and vomiting, deep and rapid breathing, dry skin and mouth, fruity breath odor, rapid and weak pulse, and low blood pressure. It can lead to coma and even death if not treated right away.

diabetic neuropathy—Damage to the nerves due to high blood sugar. Nerve damage can also be caused by conditions other than diabetes.

diabetic retinopathy—Damaged blood vessels in the eye, which can lead to blindness.

gangrene—Death of body tissue, usually caused by loss of blood flow, especially in the legs and feet.

genes—The basic units of heredity. Genes are made of DNA, a substance present in plant and animal cells that tells the cells what to do and when. Information in the genes is passed on from parent to child.

genetic engineering—A technique by which genetic material from one organism is inserted into another organism or into a foreign cell.

glaucoma—Increased pressure in the eye, which can damage the optic nerve and lead to blindness unless it is treated.

glomeruli—Tiny filters in the kidney that clean the blood.

glucagon—A hormone that raises the level of glucose in the blood. When someone has very low blood sugar, glucagon can be injected to quickly raise the blood-glucose level.

glucose—A simple sugar found in the blood. It is the body's main source of energy.

hormone—A chemical released by special cells to tell other cells what to do. For example, insulin is a hormone made by special cells in the pancreas. Insulin directs other cells to use glucose for energy.

hyperglycemia—Too high a level of glucose (sugar) in the blood. It can lead to diabetic ketoacidosis.

hypertension—High blood pressure. A condition in which the blood flows through the vessels at greater-than-normal force. It strains the heart, damages the arteries, and increases the risk of heart attack, stroke, and kidney disease.

hypoglycemia—Too low a level of glucose (sugar) in the blood. This can happen to a person with diabetes if he or she has injected too much insulin, has eaten too little food, or has exercised without extra food. The person may feel weak, shaky, nervous, sweaty, and hungry. Drinking juice or eating food containing sugar helps a low-blood-sugar reaction.

hypoglycemia unawareness—Some people may not be aware of warning signs of low blood sugar. This condition may happen after people have had many lows over a long period of time.

immune system—A complex network of cells and organs that defend the body against foreign invaders such as bacteria, viruses, or anything else that the body does not recognize as part of itself.

insulin—A hormone produced by the pancreas that helps the body use glucose.

intermittent claudication—Pain in the legs that happens when the leg muscles are not getting enough blood due to narrowing of the arteries. Walking or doing exercise brings on this kind of pain.

islet cells—Special groups of cells in the pancreas, also known as islets of Langerhans, that make and secrete several hormones that help the body use glucose. Insulin, made by the beta cells, and glucagon, made by the alpha cells, are two of these hormones.

ketones—Chemicals that the body makes when there is not enough insulin in the blood and it must break down fat for energy. Ketones can poison and kill body cells. They build up in the blood and spill out into the urine. A buildup of ketones in the body is known as ketoacidosis.

pancreas—Organ behind the stomach that contains groups of cells called the islets of Langerhans, which produce insulin and glucagon. See *islet cells*. The pancreas also secretes substances called enzymes that help the body digest food.

peripheral nerves—These are nerves that go to the arms, hands, legs, and feet.

plaque—Sticky film of germs that builds up on your teeth if you don't brush and floss every day. It can lead to gum disease.

retina—The lining at the back of the eye that records the images coming into the eye.

transient ischemic attack (TIA or mini-stroke)—Sudden weakness or numbness on one side of the body, sudden trouble talking or seeing, and sudden dizziness are some warning signs of a stroke. Sometimes one of these signs happens and disappears. This is called a TIA. Anyone who gets any of these warning signs needs to see a doctor right away.

triglyceride—Type of blood fat. The body needs insulin to remove this type of fat from the blood.

ureter—Tube that carries urine from the kidney to the bladder. Each kidney has a ureter.

veins—Blood vessels that carry blood to the heart.

Suggestions for Further Reading

Books

Becker, Gretchen. *The First Year: Type 2 Diabetes*. New York: Marlowe and Company, 2001.

Betschart, Jean, and Susan Thom. *In Control: A Guide for Teens With Diabetes*. New York: John Wiley, 1995.

Chase, Peter M. *Understanding Insulin-Dependent Diabetes, 10th Edition*. Denver, CO: Children's Diabetes Association at Denver, 2002.

Dominick, Andie. *Needles: A Memoir of Growing Up With Diabetes*. New York: Scribner, 1998.

Funnell, Martha Mitchell, and Francine Kaufman. *American Diabetes Association Complete Guide to Diabetes; The Ultimate Home Reference from the Diabetic Experts*. Third Edition, McGraw Hill, 2002.

Gregory, Adair, Carol Antoinette Peacock and Kyle Carney Gregory. *Sugar Was My Best Food*. New York: Albert Whitman, 1998.

Loy, Spike, and Bo Nasmyth Loy. *Getting a Grip on Diabetes.* New York: McGraw-Hill, 2000.

Saudek, Christopher and Richard Rubin. *The Johns Hopkins Guide to Diabetes.* Baltimore, MD: The Johns Hopkins University Press, 1997.

Swenson, Kris, and Betty Brackenridge. *Diabetes Myths, Misconceptions, and Big Fat Lies.* Tempe, AZ: Diabetes Management and Training Center, 2002.

Walsh, John, and Ruth Roberts. *Pumping Insulin.* San Diego, CA: Torrey Pines Press, 2000.

Willett, Walter C. *Eat, Drink, and Be Healthy*: *The Harvard Medical School Guide to Healthy Eating.* New York: Simon and Schuster, 2001.

Organizations and Online Sites

D.I.A.L.
The Diabetes Information and Action Line
1-800-DIABETES
The Diabetes Information and Action Line is a national network of information and referral telephone lines for people with diabetes and their families.

American Diabetes Association
1701 N. Beauregard St.
Alexandria, VA 22311
1-800-342-2383
www.diabetes.org.

Canadian Diabetes Association
15 Toronto Street, Suite 800
Toronto, Ontario M5C 2E3
www.diabetes.ca/

Centers for Disease Control and Prevention
Division of Diabetes Translation
4770 Buford Highway NE, Mailstop K-10
Atlanta, GA 30341-3717
www.cdc.gov/diabetes

Children with Diabetes Online
www.castleweb.com/diabetes

Joslin Diabetes Center
One Joslin Place
Boston, MA 02215
617-732-2400
www.joslin.harvard.edu

Juvenile Diabetes Research Foundation
120 Wall Street, 19th floor
New York, NY 10005
800-JDF-CURE
800-223-1138
www.jdrf.org

National Diabetes Information Clearinghouse (NDIC)
1 Information Way
Bethesda, MD 20893-3560
800-GETLEVEL
301-654-3327
www.niddk.nih.gov/health/diabetes/ndic.htm

National Institute of Diabetes and Digestive and Kidney
Diseases
Bldg. 31, Room 9A04
Center Drive, MSC 2560
Bethesda, MD 20892-2560
www.niddk.nih.gov

This site has cartoons about a superhero who has diabetes:
www.thehumanelement.com/courage/

Index